NATIONAL AUDUBON SOCIETY® POCKET GUIDE

A Chanticleer Press Edition

Harold A. Rehder, Zoologist Emeritus
Smithsonian Institution

Familiar Seashells

Alfred A. Knopf, New York

Prepared and produced by Chanticleer Press, Inc., New York.
Color reproductions by Nievergelt Repro AG,
Zurich, Switzerland.
Typeset by Dix Type, Inc., Syracuse, New York.
Printed and bound by Toppan Printing Co., Ltd.,
Hong Kong.

Published March 1988
Sixth printing, May 2000

Library of Congress Catalog Card Number: 87-46021
ISBN: 0-394-75795-5

Contents

How to Use This Guide

Beautiful and durable, seashells are fun to collect and easy to identify. No special techniques are required for preserving these colorful seashore objects. Learning to name them will add excitement to any trip to the beach and provide hours of pleasure at home.

Coverage — This guide covers 80 common and familiar seashells belonging to three major groups—gastropods, chitons, and bivalves. The geographical range embraces North America's seacoasts, from the shores of the Pacific to the Atlantic and along the Gulf Coast.

Organization — This easy-to-use pocket guide is divided into three parts: introductory essays and drawings; illustrated accounts of the shell species; and appendices.

Introduction — The introductory essay "What Is a Mollusk?" describes the three groups of seashells covered in the guide. "Parts of a Shell" illustrates the important features that are helpful in identification. "How Mollusks Develop and Grow" discusses the different life cycles of the animals that inhabit seashells, while "Collecting Seashells" gives tips on where to look for shells and the simple equipment useful in collecting them.

The Seashells This section includes 80 color plates, arranged visually by shape, color, and overall appearance. Opposite each illustration is a description of the shell species, its size, color, shape, and other important distinguishing features, as well as information about its range, habitat, and any similar species. An introductory paragraph provides additional information about collecting the shell, the living animal's ecology and life cycle, or its commercial value. The family or class each species belongs to is indicated by a symbol.

Appendices Following the species accounts, the appendices include the illustrated chart "Shell Groups," arranged alphabetically, with symbols for each family or class of mollusks in the guide and page numbers for the accounts of members of each group. A glossary of technical terms and an index are also featured here.

Identifying, collecting, and studying seashells can become an absorbing hobby, a pleasant outdoor pastime, or one of many sources of enjoyment on trips to the beach. Whatever effort you put into learning about seashells will be amply rewarded.

What Is a Mollusk?

Mollusks are animals without backbones, belonging to the phylum Mollusca. All mollusks have soft bodies and most have a calcareous shell consisting of either one, two, or eight parts. Next to the insects, mollusks are the most numerous group of animals on earth, with an estimated 130,000 different species. They are probably the most widely distributed group of animals, and are found on land and in fresh and salt water from the polar regions to the tropics.

The living mollusks are divided into five main groups or classes; three are represented in this guide—the gastropods, bivalves, and chitons.

Gastropods

The gastropods (class Gastropoda) comprise over 100,000 species, over three-fourths of all mollusks. The group includes the conchs, periwinkles, limpets, garden snails, and slugs. Most gastropods have shells, generally in the shape of a regular spiral consisting of numerous turns or whorls.

Typically, gastropods have a distinct head with a mouth, eyes, and sensory tentacles, and a broad foot on which they creep. Most have an organ in their throat called a radula—a series of rows of minute teeth on a flexible ribbon with which they scrape up food, tear the flesh of prey, or bore

8

holes in the shells of other mollusks. Gastropods may be plant-eaters, carnivores, scavengers, deposit-feeders (obtaining food particles from sediment), or suspension-feeders (straining suspended food particles from the water).

Bivalves The second largest mollusk group is the bivalves (class Bivalvia), including the familiar clams, oysters, and mussels. Bivalves lack a distinct head and radula, but possess a strong, hatchet-shaped foot and a shell of two roughly equal valves. The valves have one or more interlocking teeth along their upper margins and a horny ligament that operates like a spring hinge. Most bivalves burrow in sand, mud, rubble, and even wood, clay, or stone, but some, like the oysters and jingles, are attached by one of their valves to a hard surface. Others, like the mussels, attach themselves to objects with a byssus—a bundle of tough fibers. Most bivalves are suspension-feeders.

Chitons The chitons (class Polyplacophora) are among the most primitive living mollusks. They have eight oblong, shelly plates held together by muscles and a surrounding muscular girdle. Most chitons feed on algae and minute plants.

Parts of a Shell

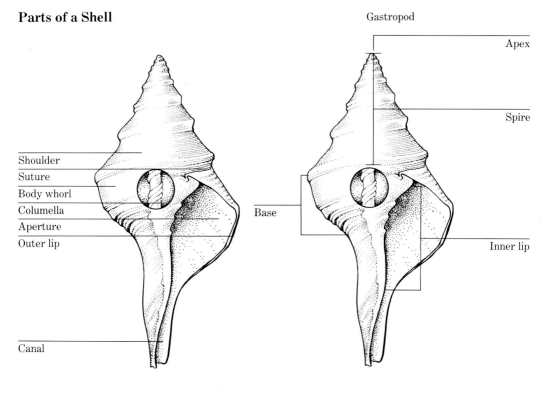

Shoulder

Suture

Body whorl

Columella

Aperture

Outer lip

Canal

Gastropod

Apex

Spire

Base

Inner lip

Bivalve

Chiton

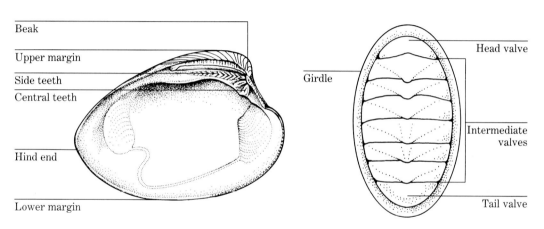

Beak

Upper margin

Side teeth

Central teeth

Hind end

Lower margin

Girdle

Head valve

Intermediate valves

Tail valve

Spiral Sculpture

Axial Sculpture

Crossed or Latticed Sculpture

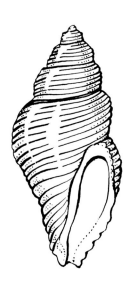

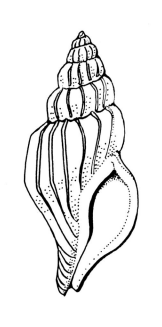

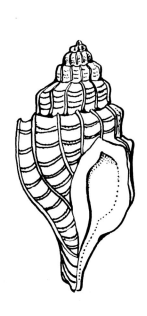

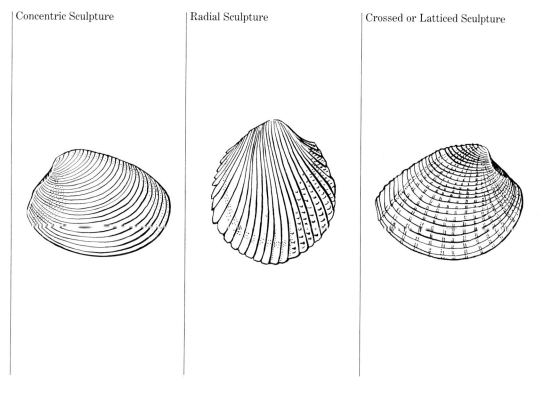

Concentric Sculpture

Radial Sculpture

Crossed or Latticed Sculpture

How Mollusks Develop and Grow

Reproduction varies greatly among the mollusks. In most, the sexes are separate, but in some, male and female are united in one animal. Slippershells begin as males, then are both male and female, and finally become females. Many species of limpets start out as males and change into females after a year or two. Most Quahogs are males at first; after a year, half become females and the rest remain males. Oysters change sex very frequently—some from females to males, others from males to females.

Fertilization

In most gastropods the eggs are fertilized by sperm inside the female's body, usually after copulation. In chitons, most bivalves, and more primitive gastropods such as limpets and topsnails, fertilization is external, and the eggs and sperm are released into the water. Some mollusks will release their eggs or sperm only in the presence of the opposite sex. In others, the males release sperm first, and this triggers the expulsion of eggs by nearby females. Some bivalves release eggs and sperm at the same time, both sexes taking their cue from the water temperature, an abundance of food, or even the phases of the moon.

Spawning

When fertilization takes place within the female, the eggs are then released directly into the water and deposited in a compact mass or thin-walled capsule whose shape depends upon the species, or the eggs are laid in long gelatinous strings. Capsules may contain many eggs, but often the smaller eggs serve as food for the larger ones, and only a few of the latter hatch. The females of a few mollusks—periwinkles, certain chitons, and some bivalves—hold the eggs in the mantle cavity, in the gills, or in a special pouch until hatching.

Young A young mollusk may hatch as a juvenile that is a miniature edition of its parents, or it may be a free-swimming veliger larva that bears little resemblance to the adult and moves through the water by means of rows of tiny, beating cilia. Young mollusks that hatch looking like minute adults settle to the bottom immediately and begin to feed, but it may be several weeks before a veliger larva sinks to the bottom. Young snails in the veliger stage have a tiny, coiled shell, and add a few whorls before settling. Young bivalves have only the beginnings of two valves. As the young mollusks feed, the body grows and new shell material forms at the outer lip in gastropods and along the edges in bivalves and chitons.

Collecting Seashells

Seashells are easy to find and collect. Anyone who strolls along a beach, particularly after a storm, and especially a beach that borders on an expanse of shallow water and sand flats, marvels at the variety of shells—many unbroken and unworn. Most shells are washed up along the high-tide line, where seaweed and debris have been left by the highest waves.

Sandbars and Mud Flats

Beaches, however, are usually a poor place to find a large variety of shells, and the experienced collector soon learns to search for shells in their natural habitats. Where sand or mud is exposed at low tide, you can collect many specimens on the flats or in pools and channels of water.

Rocky Ledges and Reefs

Many mollusks are also found on rocks, in crevices, under and on seaweed, and in rocky tidepools. In tropical areas, coral reef flats and the many tidepools and sandy patches near them offer an abundance of marine mollusks, especially if you turn over loose coral rocks and slabs. Always remember to replace these rocks in their original positions.

Equipment

Collecting equipment should be kept to the minimum. You'll need a pail or a mesh bag—fine enough to prevent specimens from falling through and made so that it can be fastened to your belt or swimming trunks. You can also use this bag to hold smaller bags, plastic vials, and jars for delicate or small shells. If you are collecting in sand or mud, bring along a small digging tool. If you will be in a coral or rocky area, also bring along a small hammer, a crowbar, and a knife for prying up limpets and chitons. Long forceps are handy for removing mollusks from crevices. In lagoons, deep pools, and in areas of reduced surf, a face mask and snorkel are indispensible for collecting and revealing the beauty and wealth of life found in tropical waters. Another useful piece of equipment is the "lookbox"—a square, watertight box with an open top and a clear plastic bottom. You can use it to examine clearly the bottoms of pools, channels, and other areas where you wouldn't or couldn't snorkel.

Cleaning Shells — Most shells should be cleaned to avoid disagreeable odors. Place them in a pot of cold water and bring it to a boil. Let the water boil for five minutes (small, thin shells need less time), and then let the pot cool gradually.

The Seashells

Purple Dwarf Olive *Olivella biplicata*

Native Americans of central California once used this shell to make necklaces and to decorate their clothing. Like other members of the genus *Olivella* and the larger species of *Oliva*, the Purple Dwarf Olive is a carnivorous scavenger. During the day it lies buried in the sand, but at twilight it emerges to feed on animal remains.

Identification ½–1½″ high. Stout and broadly ovate with conical spire and large, smooth body whorl. Glossy brownish-gray to almost white, with a fine dark line below the suture and narrow brown band above spiral, thickening at base. Aperture elongately triangular; outer lip thin, flaring at base; inner lip has thickened fold at base with 2–4 spiral ridges.

Range Vancouver Island, British Columbia, to Baja California.

Habitat On sand, from low-tide line to water 150′ deep.

Lettered Olive *Oliva sayana*

The olive family is a favorite among collectors because the glossy, cylindrical shells exist in many different colors and patterns. These carnivores burrow in search of small crustaceans or bivalves, enveloping the prey with their foot and feeding at leisure under the sand. As the animal burrows, its fleshy mantle and foot extend to cover the shell, thus preserving its gloss.

Identification 1¾–2¾″ high. Cylindrical; body whorl large; spire small, conical, pointed, with a narrow channel separating the whorls. Glossy, grayish or yellowish with irregular reddish-brown zigzag markings and 2 broad, indistinct dark bands. Aperture long, narrow; lower part of inner lip white, with slanting spiral ridges.

Range North Carolina to Texas and Brazil.

Habitat In sand, from low-tide line to deep water.

22

California Cone *Conus californicus*

This species belongs to the large cone family, whose members are found all over the world in tropical and warm-temperate seas. All are carnivorous, and can be divided into three groups according to what they eat— other snails, worms, or small fish. The California Cone preys mainly on snails but may also feed on worms. It overpowers its victims by piercing them with a harpoonlike tooth and then injecting poison.

Identification ¾–1⅝" high. Ovate, conical; spire low, the whorls with bluntly angled shoulders; knobby ridge below suture; body whorl smooth except for obscure spiral threads that become stronger toward base. Yellowish-brown with faint white band on shoulder; covered with a thin brown skin. Aperture narrow above, wider below.

Range San Francisco to S. Baja California.

Habitat In sand or rubble, from low-tide line to water 100′ deep.

24

Scotch Bonnet *Semicassis granulata*

Members of the helmet snail family, to which the Scotch
Bonnet belongs, are all found in warm seas. Most species
have a large body whorl with a shieldlike thickening that
extends from the inner lip. These animals feed on sea
urchins and sand dollars found in sand. The females lay
their egg capsules in irregular masses or in towerlike
shapes. Some of the larger species are eaten, and in the
South Pacific the shells have been used as cooking
utensils. Certain species are still used to make cameos.

Identification 1–3½" high. Broadly ovate. Yellowish-white to white,
with 3 or more spiral rows of brownish spots on the last
whorl, which often bears spiral grooves but is sometimes
smooth. Inner wall of aperture thickened, shieldlike,
freestanding, and roughened at its lower part; outer lip
thickened and toothed.

Range North Carolina to Texas and Brazil.

Habitat On sand in shallow water.

Atlantic Dogwinkle *Nucella lapillus*

Dogwinkles are related to the murex snails; members of both families are found on and under rocks and coral reefs in all oceans. Most are of medium size and are carnivores, feeding on various forms of marine life. Many species have a gland in the mantle that produces a fluid for anesthetizing prey. At first yellowish, on exposure to sunlight this substance turns deep purple; it is the source of the dye used by ancient Mediterranean peoples to make the "royal purple" of their ceremonial robes.

Identification 1–2″ high. Thick, ovate, with pointed apex. Varies from white to reddish-brown. Numerous low spiral ridges may be knobby or scaly. Aperture ovate; yellowish or brown inside; inner lip broad, somewhat flattened; outer lip thick, flaring.

Range Newfoundland to New York; also Europe.

Habitat On rocks between tide lines, often among seaweed.

Channeled Nassa *Nassarius fossatus*

Often called the Giant Western Nassa, this species is the largest and one of the most common nassas on the Pacific Coast. To collect these active scavengers, place a dead fish in shallow water; in a short time the nassas, their keen sensory organs stimulated, can be seen heading for the bait from as far away as 50 feet or more.

Identification 1¼–2″ high. Comparatively large, ovate, with relatively high, pointed spire. Yellowish-gray to pale reddish-brown or orange-brown. Spire whorls moderately convex, body whorl well rounded, all marked by spiral ridges that are beaded where they cross narrow axial riblets; riblets become obscure on lower part of body whorl. Aperture ovate, outer lip toothed at margin and ridged inside.

Range Vancouver Island, British Columbia, to central Baja California.

Habitat On sand and mud, from low-tide line to water 60′ deep.

Three-lined Nassa *Nassarius trivittatus*

This common species is also known as the New England Basket Whelk and the New England Dog Whelk. The animal is whitish with pale violet spots. It is abundant on intertidal sand flats where it feeds as a scavenger. This dog whelk also preys on the "sand collar" egg capsules of the Common Northern Moonsnail, and even lays its own vase-shaped, many-sided egg capsules on those of the moonsnail.

Identification ½–⅞″ high. Elongately ovate, with high, conical spire. Yellowish-gray; southern specimens sometimes have 3 narrow, spiraling, reddish-brown lines on body whorl. Whorls strongly angled at top making for a deep suture and giving shell a stepped appearance; whorls have strong axial riblets, with 4–6 equal beaded spiral ridges. Aperture ovate, ending below in a short canal; inner lip with thin, shelly glaze.

Range Canada to NE. Florida.

Habitat On sand and muddy sand, between tide lines and deeper.

Emarginate Dogwinkle *Nucella emarginata*

In contrast to the Atlantic Coast, where only one dogwinkle species, the Atlantic Dogwinkle, is found, the Pacific Coast has four, all of them abundant on its rocks. These species vary considerably in sculpture and color. The females lay their eggs in vase-shaped capsules that are attached by a short stalk to rocks and to the undersides of stones. After four months the young crawl out of the capsules.

Identification   ⅞–1⅛″ high. Broadly ovate, with short spire and large body whorl. Yellowish to dark brown, sometimes banded. Whorls with irregular spiral ridges that are sometimes knobby, alternating with finer ridges. Aperture large, oval, yellowish to brownish inside; outer lip somewhat flaring and wavy.

Range   Alaska to N. Baja California.

Habitat   Between tide lines on rocks and in crevices, often near mussel beds.

34

Bruised Nassa *Nassarius vibex*

This member of the dog whelk family is also known as the Mottled Dog Whelk or Eastern Dog Whelk and is readily distinguished by the presence of a thickened shelly layer that extends from the inner lip over the adjacent part of the last whorl. It has been observed feeding on the egg cases of worms. The females lay their eggs in flattened, stalked capsules from which the free-swimming young emerge.

Identification   ⅜–¾″ high. Stout, broadly ovate, with pointed spire. Gray, often with spiral bands or spirally arranged reddish-brown spots. Whorls with strong, rounded ribs crossed by spiral cords. Aperture oval; inner lip area covered by a white, shelly layer, especially on lower part of body whorl.

Range   Cape Cod, Massachusetts, to Florida and Mexico.

Habitat   On sand near low-tide line.

True Tulip *Fasciolaria tulipa*

Members of the spindle, or tulip, shell family are carnivorous, feeding on other snails and bivalves. The female lays its eggs in cone-shaped, horny capsules attached by the narrow end to rocks and shells. Tulip shells are moderately large and broadly spindle-shaped, with the body whorl prolonged at the base into a slender canal.

Identification 2½–9½″ high. Broadly spindle-shaped. Grayish-white, yellowish-white, or grayish-green, usually with many fine lines and brown to orange axial splotches. Body whorl smooth or with many fine spiral ridges, especially on base and on long basal canal. Outer lip finely and sharply toothed, with spiral ridges inside.

Range North Carolina to Texas and West Indies.

Habitat On sand and mud, intertidal zone to deeper water.

Common Northern Whelk *Buccinum undatum*

The whelks form the largest and most varied family of mollusks, its species inhabiting all waters from the Arctic and Antarctic to the tropics, from shoreline to depths of 15,000 feet. Those like the Common Northern Whelk, found in cooler and deeper waters, tend to be of medium to large size and have a thin to moderately thick shell; those from warm climes are smaller and have thicker shells. All are predators or scavengers. Some northern whelk species have been eaten in Europe for thousands of years.

Identification 1½–5½″ high. Medium size, broadly ovate. Shell moderately thick, whitish-yellow to pale brown. Whorls rounded, with broad, curved axial ribs crossed by spiral ridges; fresh shells covered by a thin, papery skin. Aperture broadly ovate, white, with broad notch or canal at the base.

Range Arctic waters to New Jersey; also Europe.

Habitat On rocks and sand, from low-tide line to deep water.

Channeled Whelk *Busycon canaliculata*

Bushel baskets of these whelks were once commonly sold as food in the markets of Boston. This species differs from the Knobbed Whelk in being somewhat smaller and lighter in weight, and in having flattened egg capsules that resemble a change purse rather than a pillbox. Although most Busycon whelks coil to the right, some coil to the left—a phenomenon that may be constant for a species or subspecies.

Identification   3½–7½" high. Large, broadly ovate. Whorls with sharp angle at shoulder; beaded with numerous small knobs, the knobs often obscure on last whorl and with a pronounced channel at upper margin, just below the preceding whorl. Aperture yellowish to brown inside, ending in a fairly long, open canal.

Range   Cape Cod, Massachusetts, to N. Florida; introduced into San Francisco Bay.

Habitat   In sand or mud, from between tide lines to deeper water.

42

Knobbed Whelk *Busycon carica*

These rather large, carnivorous snails feed on clams. The whelk grasps a clam with its large muscular foot, pulls the victim's valves slightly apart, and wedges the edge of its shell's outer lip between the clam's valves. The female lays a series of pillbox-shaped capsules that are attached to a fibrous strand; these are frequently found on beaches. Busycon whelks, a group of six species (and possibly several subspecies), live along the Atlantic Coast of North America.

Identification 4–9″ high. Rather heavy, with low, conical spire and large body, narrowing below to a short, broad, spoutlike canal, a prolongation of the aperture. Whorls angled above, with a series of knobs on the angle. Grayish-white to pale brownish, with dark axial streaks. Aperture whitish to orange inside.

Range Cape Cod, Massachusetts, to Cape Canaveral, Florida.

Habitat In sand, from shallow water to 15′ deep.

Pink Conch *Strombus gigas*

The Pink Conch is a great favorite of collectors because of its size and pink color of the aperture and the inside of its broad outer lip. Like many other conch species, it has long been a source of food for the inhabitants of southern Florida and the West Indies, and is still a common item on the menus of Florida restaurants. The young of the species lack the expanded lip, and have strong spines on the relatively high spire. Also known as the Queen Conch, this is the largest of the wing conch family found in North America.

Identification 7–12″ high. Large, heavy; adults with a large body whorl and a greatly expanded outer lip. Aperture pink inside and glossy pink or white on thickened outer lip. Spire broadly conical, the whorls knobbed, the knobs becoming spines on the body whorl. Exterior has a thin brown skin that easily flakes off.

Range Florida Keys, where it is now rare, to Venezuela.

Habitat In sand and rubble, in water 5–15′ deep; generally amid eelgrass.

Florida Fighting Conch *Strombus alatus*

The wing conchs are a family of medium-size to large shells found in tropical waters. Prized by collectors because of their size, distinctive form, and coloring, many are characterized by a broad, winglike outer lip. They live in sand or rubble, especially among sea grasses, and feed on algae. The animal uses its narrow, pointed operculum, a trapdoor that closes the aperture, as a canelike lever to propel itself across the sand, and also as a weapon against predators.

Identification 2¾–4¼″ high. Thick, broadly ovate, with knobs on spire becoming spines on last whorl. Yellowish to reddish-brown, often mottled with dark zigzag stripes. Aperture purplish-brown and orange inside, inner wall with brownish glaze; outer lip winglike, angled above and with a broad, shallow notch below.

Range North Carolina to Texas.

Habitat In shallow water in sandy areas near marine grasses; abundant in Florida on sandbars and sand flats.

Florida Crown Conch *Melongena corona*

This species is one of the three crown conchs, all of which are found in tropical American waters. They are mainly scavengers but also feed occasionally on various kinds of mollusks. The female lays disk-shaped egg capsules in a row on rocks or dead shells. In about four weeks the tiny crawling young emerge. The Florida Crown Conch varies quite a bit in size, shape, and sculpture, and a number of varieties or subspecies have been given names.

Identification   1–8″ high. Broadly ovate or elongate; spire broadly conical or turreted. White with brown spiral bands. Whorls strongly shouldered, with channeled shelf and row of spines at shoulder; rows of spines may be present also on side of body whorl and base. Aperture ovate, canal at base broad and open.

Range   Florida and Alabama.

Habitat   In mud or sand in bays and lagoons, from between tide lines to water 6′ deep.

Frilled Dogwinkle *Nucella lamellosa*

This is the most variable of the dogwinkles; some specimens are almost smooth, and others may have leafy axial frills and spiral ridges. The smoother, thicker-shelled specimens are found where there are many waves while those with thinner shells and with frills and spines are found in quieter waters.

Identification   1–3¼" high. Ovate to elongately ovate. White to light brown, sometimes banded. Whorls may be thick-shelled and more or less smooth or spirally ridged; or they may be less thick and have thin axial ribs with spines where they cross spiral ridges; axial ribs may become erect and frilly. Aperture ovate; inner lip broad, white, outer lip rather broad and flared, usually with 3 broad, knoblike teeth.

Range   Alaska to central California.

Habitat   On rocks, especially in sheltered places, from between tide lines to just below low-tide line.

Foliate Thornmouth *Ceratostoma foliatum*

This striking member of the murex family has also been called the Leafy Thorn Purpura. The shells seem to vary in color and size according to locality; those from Puget Sound and northward are larger and darker, while those from Oregon and California are generally white and smaller. In some places in Oregon they are banded with brown. The species feeds on bivalves.

Identification 1¾–3⅜″ high. Large, ovate. Spire elevated, conical, last 2 whorls with 3 large, leaflike, wavy flanges that are closely and finely ridged on front side; on back side and between flanges are several strong spiral ridges that may be knobby on the whorl. White, yellowish, or pale brown, often with brown bands. Aperture ovate; inner and outer lips margined and freestanding; outer tip toothed, with spine near base; canal covered and twisted at end.

Range Alaska to S. California.

Habitat On and among rocks, intertidal zone to water 10′ or deeper.

Circled Rocksnail *Ocenebra circumtexta*

The members of the Ocenebra group of rocksnails have also been called Dwarf Tritons. Like their relatives the drills, they feed on clams and other bivalves by drilling a hole in the victim's shell and sucking up the soft parts with their long snout or proboscis. They belong to the large murex family.

Identification ½–1″ high. Broadly ovate, thick, with well-rounded whorls, the last strongly rounded and narrowed at base. Whorls have strong, rounded axial ribs crossed by spiral ridges that are rather broad on body whorl, separated by deep, narrow grooves; when fresh, spiral ridges may show fine axial threads that are more prominent in the grooves. White to grayish-white, with 2 spiral bands of dark brown blotches on body whorl. Aperture ovate; outer lip somewhat flaring and toothed inside.

Range Monterey, California, to central Baja California.

Habitat On rocks, especially in crevices, between tide lines.

Poulson Rocksnail *Roperia poulsoni*

The Latin name of this genus commemorates Edward W. Roper, an amateur California conchologist of the late 19th century. Also known as Poulson Dwarf Triton, the species was once placed in the genus *Ocenebra*. It is the most common and largest of the Ocenebra shell group in California and, because of its size and the decorative spiral markings, is a favorite with collectors.

Identification 1–2" high. Elongately ovate, rather thick-shelled, with 8–9 broad axial ribs per whorl. Whitish, with several broad, rounded spiral ridges that are knobby where they cross axial ribs; many fine reddish-brown incised lines between white spiral ridges. Aperture ovate, white, ending in a short, open canal; several teeth inside outer lip.

Range Santa Barbara, California, to S. Baja California.

Habitat On rocks and pilings, from between tide lines to just below low-tide line.

Thick-lipped Drill *Eupleura caudata*

Related to shells in the murex family, this and some other species called drills are found on oyster beds, where they prey on oysters by drilling holes in their shells so that they can feed on the soft parts. Drills can do considerable damage to commercial beds. To control the drills, traps with live young oysters have been used, as have chemical repellants.

Identification   ½–1½″ high. Small, with pointed apex and angled whorls; sculpted with spiral ridges and axial ribs. Last whorl has compressed, erect rib on each side, giving shell a flattened appearance. Aperture ovate, outer lip with 6 small teeth on inside; canal almost closed, projecting below the aperture.

Range   S. Massachusetts to S. Florida.

Habitat   On oyster beds in shallow water.

Angulate Wentletrap *Epitonium angulatum*

The wentletrap family consists of several hundred species found worldwide. Usually white, the high-spired shells have numerous rounded whorls with axial ribs. Wentletraps are carnivorous, most feeding on sea anemones or corals; many of them live in close association with sea anemones. The female lays egg capsules in a string covered with sand grains or mud.

Identification ½–⅞″ high. Elongate, white, with many rounded, glossy whorls narrowly separated from one another; 9–10 thin, bladelike ribs, usually angled, especially on whorls near apex. Aperture oval to round, surrounded by a thickened lip.

Similar Species Humphreys Wentletrap (*E. humphreysii*), ½–⅞″ high, is more slender, not shiny, with thicker ribs; found in same range.

Range New York to Florida and Texas.

Habitat In sand and rubble, and near sea anemones, in shallow water. Often found in tidal drift on beaches.

62

California Hornsnail *Cerithidea californica*

Members of the hornsnail family are found only in brackish water, in estuaries and mangrove swamps. Some of them are practically amphibious, climbing trees three to five feet above the muddy bottom. One species can survive being out of water for as long as two weeks. Female hornsnails lay egg capsules in long, jellylike strings covered with grains of mud. The California Hornsnail is very abundant on mud flats, where it spends much time in pools and channels. In San Francisco Bay, the eggs and young are preyed upon by the introduced Eastern Mudsnail *(Ilynassa obsoleta)*.

Identification 1–1¾″ high. Elongate, high-spired; whorls rounded with many strong axial ribs crossed by weak spiral threads; 1–2 broad yellowish to brownish axial ribs on spire. Brown with several white bands. Aperture round, outer lip broad and flaring.

Range Central California to Gulf of California.

Habitat On intertidal mud flats in bays and estuaries.

Carinate Dovesnail *Alia carinata*

Although dovesnails are found in shallow waters worldwide, the feeding habits of only a few species are known. It appears that most of them feed on algae, but some may be carnivorous. The females lay their eggs in pillbox-shaped capsules. A small amphipod crustacean that lives among colonies of the Carinate Dovesnail mimics it in shape, size, and color.

Identification ¼–⅜″ high. Small, with elongate, pointed spire. Pale brown, often with spiral bands of reddish-brown and white spots, which may be arranged axially, and sometimes with a white spiral band. Whorls generally smooth, body whorl angled at shoulder; angle strongest at aperture. Aperture white or pinkish-white inside, outer lip dark brown inside with strong teeth; often brown outside also.

Range S. Alaska to S. Baja California.

Habitat Among grasses and algae, from low-tide line to water 15′ deep.

Checkered Periwinkle *Littorina scutulata*

All periwinkles can withdraw completely into their shells and close the aperture tightly with a trapdoor, called the operculum. The periwinkle's foot is divided longitudinally. When progressing over the rocks, the animal moves one side of the foot forward first and then moves the other side. This species lays its eggs in floating capsules.

Identification   ⅜–½″ high. Elongately ovate, with moderately convex whorls. Smooth, light to dark reddish-brown, with white spots arranged in axially slanting rows. Inner lip narrow.

Similar Species   Eroded Periwinkle *(L. keenae)*, ½–¾″ high, is larger and broader, brownish-gray with white spots, but generally eroded; Puget Sound to Baja California.

Range   Alaska to Baja California.

Habitat   Between tide lines, on and among rocks and algae.

Common Periwinkle *Littorina littorea*

The periwinkle family comprises over a hundred species. Found in all oceans, periwinkles occur from low-tide level to well above high water on rocks, marine structures, and vegetation in marshes and swamps. Here they feed by scraping off algae and other small plant life with their well-developed radula, an organ with minute teeth. Periwinkles are generally small, conical shells with a thin, horny trapdoor, or operculum. The Common Periwinkle has been used as food in Europe since ancient times and is still gathered and eaten boiled in rural areas.

Identification To 1″ high. Small, thick, broadly oval, with low spire. Gray or brownish-gray, sometimes with white spiral bands. Rather smooth, although young and unworn shells may show fine, spiral ridges. Aperture oval; dark brown inside, inner lip white.

Range Labrador to Maryland; also Europe.

Habitat Intertidal zone, on rocks and other structures.

70

Blue Topsnail *Calliostoma ligatum*

Also called the Western Ribbed Topshell, this species gets its name from the pearly bluish color revealed when the top shell layer is worn away. All members of the topsnail family have pearly shells that generally remain hidden beneath a thin, shelly layer, but the lustrous undersurface is apparent inside the aperture and wherever the outer layer is eroded.

Identification ¾–1″ high. Broadly conical, almost as wide as high. Thick-shelled; whorls gently convex, encircled by strong, light-colored spiral cords or ridges. Dark yellow to brownish-yellow, sometimes with dark spots below suture. Body whorl bluntly angled, base flat, no umbilicus.

Range Alaska to central California.

Habitat Intertidal zone, among algae and under rocks.

Marsh Periwinkle *Littoraria irrorata*

This thick-shelled, grayish-white snail is found in abundance crawling on marsh grasses and other vegetation above the high-water mark in the salt marshes and estuaries of our Middle Atlantic and southeastern states. Like the Common Periwinkle and other members of the periwinkle family, the Marsh Periwinkle grazes on minute plant life and lays horny egg capsules that float in the water. The young leave the capsules as swimming larvae.

Identification   ¾–1¼" high. Broadly ovate, with flat-sided whorls and pointed spire. Grayish-white, sculptured with low, spiral ridges marked with reddish-brown streaks. Inner lip brown; outer lip thin with short, red-brown streaks on inside margin.

Range   New York to central Florida, and on Gulf Coast from Florida to Texas.

Habitat   On and among vegetation in marshy areas and estuaries.

Bleeding Tooth *Nerita peloronta*

The nerite family is found throughout the warm regions of the world in salt- and freshwater habitats. The marine species occur in large numbers between tide lines, where they feed on algae. The animal can seal itself in its shell with a flat, shelly operculum, or trapdoor, which is often grainy on the outside and has a peglike projection on the inner edge. The female lays her eggs in single, horny, dome-shaped or flattened capsules. This species, which gets its common name from the bloodlike stain near its teeth, is a great favorite with collectors because of its color.

Identification ¾–1½" high. Roundish. Spiral ridges on whorls below apex becoming obscure on large, last whorl. Grayish-white with black and red zigzag streaks. Inner lip broad, flattened, toothed at edge, with orange or scarlet blotch above teeth.

Range SE. Florida and the West Indies.

Habitat On rocks, at or near low-tide line.

76

Black Tegula *Tegula funebralis*

Most of the tegula topsnails found in the cooler waters of our Pacific Coast occur in great numbers. Like all topsnails, tegulas have a round, flexible, horny operculum, or trapdoor. The Black Tegula animal is almost completely black. These vegetarians feed on algae or decaying vegetable matter. They are hosts to the tiny Black Limpet *(Collisella asmi)*, which is found almost exclusively on the last whorl of the Black Tegula.

Identification ¾–1¾" high. Solid, thick-shelled, varying from low and dome-shaped to conical. Whorls purplish-black, apex often eroded; smooth except for several spiral ridges below suture, upper ridge scaly. White area at center of base; aperture nearly circular with 2 small nodules at base of inner lip.

Similar Species Brown Tegula *(Tegula brunnea)*, 1–1½" high, is similar but pale brown with a brownish-white base; Oregon to S. California.

Range Vancouver, British Columbia, to Baja California.

Habitat On rocks between tide lines.

Shark Eye *Neverita duplicata*

Common on the beaches of the southeastern and Gulf
states, this member of the moonsnail family varies in
shape; some specimens have a rather high spire.
Apparently diet can influence the color of the shelly pad
found on the underside. The dark apical whorls
surrounded by paler ones give this shell its common
name. It preys on clams and other bivalves that it finds
in the sand. First the moonsnail bores into the bivalve,
then it feeds on the soft tissue.

Identification 7/8–3″ high. Dome-shaped, usually wider than high.
Smooth, bluish-gray to brownish-gray, apical whorls
darker, base generally paler; umbilicus broad, mostly
covered by a whitish to brown pad.

Range Massachusetts to Florida and Gulf States.

Habitat In sand, intertidal zone to just below low-tide line.

Common Northern Moonsnail *Polinices heros*

The moonsnail family comprises several hundred species found worldwide. Moonsnails typically have either a horny or shelly operculum, or trapdoor, and a large, muscular foot, with which they actively burrow in sand. At feeding time these carnivores make a clean round hole in a clam's shell with their radula and suck up the victim's soft parts. Females lay egg capsules in thin, flattened, spiral bands of sand grains held together by mucous, which, when dried and hardened, form the "sand collars" found on beaches.

Identification 1½–5″ high. Almost round, with low, pointed spire. Smooth, grayish-white to brownish-gray. Aperture semicircular; outer lip thin, glossy and brownish inside; inner lip whitish, partly expanded at lower end over narrow umbilicus. Operculum horny.

Range Gulf of St. Lawrence, Canada, to North Carolina.

Habitat In sand, intertidal zone or deeper in southern part of range.

Lewis Moonsnail *Polinices lewisii*

This is the largest living moonsnail and is most commonly found in the summer months. It has a relatively small, brown-stained shelly pad, or callus, that partly covers the umbilicus. When the animal crawls about underwater or burrows in the sand, fleshy extensions of the foot may cover the shell, making it look like a huge slug. A mound of sand often camouflages the presence of this large moonsnail.

Identification 2¼–5½″ high. Large, almost round, thick. Yellowish-white to light brown, base often paler. Whorls slightly flattened below suture. Umbilicus narrow, partially covered by a shelly callus stained with brown. Aperture almost semicircular.

Range Vancouver Island, British Columbia, to N. Baja California.

Habitat On sand in bays, intertidal zone to water 600′ deep.

Atlantic Slippershell *Crepidula fornicata*

Shaped like slippers or boats, these shells make favorite play objects for children on the beach. Slippershells are arched or flattened, with the apex at one end and a flat shelf underneath that helps protect the animal's soft organs. The prominent shelf in this species explains its other common names, Boatshell and Quarterdeck. Since the animals rarely move, they feed on minute particles brought to them by water currents. They live on rocks or on other shells; sometimes many of the same species, one piled on top of another, form a chain.

Identification   ¾–2½″ long. Back arched, oval in outline, apex curved downward at one end. Surface smooth, yellowish-white with brown blotches or radiating lines. Interior white, shiny, sometimes marked with brown; shelf with curved edge covers about half of hind end.

Range   Canada to Florida and Texas; introduced into Washington State and Europe.

Habitat   Intertidal zone, on rocks, shells, or horseshoe crabs.

86

Lined Chiton *Tonicella lineata*

The chitons are a group of primitive mollusks that have a shell made of eight overlapping plates held together by muscles and an encircling muscular girdle. The girdle may be naked and leathery, or covered with shelly scales, or spicules, or may have tufts of bristles. The animals have a broad foot, on which they creep about at night over the rocks browsing for food—mainly algae and other minute plants. They can cling tenaciously to rocks, making it difficult to pry them loose.

Identification   1–2″ long. Oblong or oval. Valves reddish-brown to orange-red, diagonal blackish-brown lines edged with white on sides; more or less concentric lines on head and tail valves. Girdle smooth and leathery.

Range   Alaska to S. California, where it is uncommon.

Habitat   On rocky shores, at or below low-tide line; the young live deeper, migrating toward shore as adults.

Black Katy *Katharina tunicata*

The Black Katy has a broad, black leathery girdle that covers most of the shelly valves, but some other chitons have even more extensive girdles that leave only a small part of each valve exposed. The Giant Pacific Chiton *(Cryptochiton stelleri)*, up to 13 inches long, has a reddish-brown girdle that completely covers the valves. The Black Katy is not sensitive to light and often feeds on algae during the day. It is named for Lady Katharine Douglas, who sent shells from the Northwest Coast to the British Museum in the early 1800s.

Identification 1½–3″ long. Moderately large, elongately ovate. Exposed portion of valves usually eroded, but when fresh, grayish-brown with fine, crowded lines of beads. Girdle broad, black or brown, covering more than half of valves and encroaching deeply between valves. Foot reddish or salmon-colored.

Range Alaska to Monterey, California.

Habitat On rocks, often among seaweed, from between tide lines to just below low-tide line.

Black Abalone *Haliotis cracherodii*

The abalone family consists of dish- or ear-shaped spiral shells with a large body whorl. They are pearly or iridescent on the inside and have a series of holes along the outer margin, through which water and wastes are expelled. With their large, muscular foot, abalones cling tenaciously to rocks, feeding on algae, including the giant kelp, and not moving very far from home base. The Black Abalone is the most common abalone in California but is of little commercial value because of its small size and undesirable dark meat.

Identification 3–6″ long. Broadly oval. Exterior bluish or greenish-black, generally smooth, with 5–8 holes flush with surface. Interior pearly white with pinkish or greenish flecks and dark border at edge.

Range Central Oregon to Baja California.

Habitat On rocks, intertidal zone to water 20′ deep.

Red Abalone *Haliotis rufescens*

The largest and most commercially important abalone, this species is the one most often served in restaurants. Native Americans not only ate abalone but also fashioned ornaments from the shells; today the iridescent interior is still utilized in the manufacture of jewelry and trinkets. At the present time the taking of abalones in California by commercial divers and collectors is strictly controlled. Sea otters, octopus, and other marine animals are their natural predators.

Identification 8–12″ long. Broadly oval, somewhat flattened. Exterior reddish with broad wavy ridges crossed by fine spiral threads; 3–4 holes on outer margin have slightly raised edges. Interior highly iridescent, tinged with pink, pale blue, or pale green, large muscle scar in center; narrow, reddish border on margin.

Range Oregon to central Baja California; most abundant in S. California.

Habitat On rocks, from between tide lines to water 540′ deep; abundant in water 20–40′ deep.

Rough Keyhole Limpet *Diodora aspera*

The keyhole limpets are a family of conical, cap-shaped, or flattened shells with either a hole at the top or front side, or a slit or notch at the front end. They have a broad foot on which they creep at night, browsing for food on algae-covered rocks. Water is taken in under the edge of the shell, passes over the gills, and then is expelled through the hole or slit along with waste matter. Besides the species described here, numerous others are found in the warmer waters of our coasts. Some are commonly used in shellcraft.

Identification   1–2¾″ long. Broadly oval in outline, with broad, oval hole somewhat in front of middle. Exterior grayish-white or yellow with numerous dark radial rays and many rough, narrow radial ridges crossed by finer concentric threads. Interior white, with thickened margin around hole, squared off at hind end; inner edge of shell finely grooved.

Range   Alaska to Baja California.

Habitat   On rocks at low-tide line.

96

Masked Limpet *Notoacmaea persona*

Unlike keyhole limpets, members of the limpet family do not have a hole or groove in the shell. The Masked Limpet, abundant on our West Coast, is found frequently in rock crevices where there are strong waves. The Latin species name means "mask," to which the shell's internal brown blotch bears a fanciful resemblance.

Identification 1–1⅞″ long. Oval in outline, moderately elevated, with apex in front of middle. Exterior bluish or brownish-gray, with white spots and often with white radial lines in lower half; smooth or with fine radiating riblets. Interior white to bluish with irregular central brown spot; margin dark brown, sometimes with white spots.

Similar Species Pacific Plate Limpet *(N. scutum)*, 1–2⅜″ long, is more elliptical to almost round, with a lower, more central apex and a paler, more irregular internal brown spot; Alaska to Baja California.

Range Alaska to central California.

Habitat Intertidal zone, on sheltered rocks or in crevices.

Fingered Limpet *Collisella digitalis*

This is one of the most common limpets on the California coast. Its scientific name, which means "fingerlike," refers to the broad, rounded ribs of the arched shell. Most limpets have a strong homing instinct, returning to their original settlement place after a night of moving about feeding on algae. They scrape the algae from the rocks by means of their strong radula, a ribbonlike organ with rows of curved teeth.

Identification $\quad$ ¾–1⅜" long. Base oval, apex near front end; back arched, convex, with broad ridges from apex to shell edge. Dark greenish-gray to reddish-brown, with irregular white streaks or spots. Interior whitish or bluish-white with brown blotch in middle; margin wavy, blackish-brown.

Range $\quad$ Alaska to Baja California.

Habitat $\quad$ On vertical rocks in intertidal zone, where there are waves.

Atlantic Plate Limpet *Notoacmaea testudinalis*

Like other members of the limpet family, this species lives on shoreline rocks and marine plants, and is especially abundant along the coast of Maine. At night it becomes active, moving about and feeding on algae and other minute plant life. With its broad, muscular foot, a limpet adheres firmly to rocks to withstand waves and can be pried loose only with difficulty.

Identification   ⅞–1¾″ long. Broadly oval in outline, moderately high, with central apex. Exterior fairly smooth but often with fine radial striations; grayish-white and usually streaked with brown. Interior whitish to bluish with brown blotch in center and small brown markings around internal border.

Range   Arctic seas to Long Island Sound, New York; also N. Europe.

Habitat   Usually on rocks between tide lines; a thin, elongate form is found on eelgrass.

Owl Limpet *Lottia gigantea*

The Owl Limpet is the largest limpet found in North America. It is sometimes polished and used as jewelry. Like all members of the limpet family, it has a broad foot on which it creeps about at night grazing on rocks or marine plants. Females lay eggs in a mucous layer on rocks; these hatch rapidly as free-swimming larvae that eventually settle on the bottom.

Identification 1¾–4¼″ long. Broadly oval in outline, relatively low, with apex near front end; front end slightly narrower than hind end. Exterior brownish with white blotches, usually in a radial or netted pattern; most conspicuous in young shells, near margin in adults. Interior shiny, bluish-white blotched with brown, margin wide, dark brown.

Range N. Washington to central Baja Cailfornia.

Habitat On rocks near high-tide line in spray zone.

Blue Mussel *Mytilus edulis*

The Blue Mussel is probably the most frequently eaten bivalve after the oyster and the scallop. Like the oyster, it is grown commercially, especially along the Atlantic shore of France, where mussel farms have long been established. In this country it is still a largely untapped source of food. All mussel species attach themselves to rock, coral, other shells, or wood by means of a bundle of hairlike strands called a byssus.

Identification 1¼–4″ long. Ovate, rather thin-shelled, fan-shaped, with beaks at front end, hind end rounded; upper margin angled, lower margin almost straight. Exterior smooth, bluish-gray, covered with a thin, tough but smooth, dark brown to bluish-black skin. Interior bluish-white. Horny hinge ligament holding valves together is on internal shelf behind pointed beaks; 4–7 small teeth at front end.

Range Arctic to South Carolina, and Alaska to Baja California; also in Europe.

Habitat Attached to rocks and wooden structures near low-tide line.

106

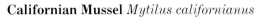

Californian Mussel *Mytilus californianus*

This is the largest species of the mussel family occurring in North America. Its shape varies according to habitat: Larger, more elongated specimens are found in exposed localities, while smaller, broader ones live in sheltered bays. Californian Mussels are edible but are gathered only in the cooler months, because in summer they ingest large numbers of marine organisms whose poisonous excretions in the bivalves' gills can cause illness in humans.

Identification 2–10″ long. Elongately ovate, inflated, with front end pointed and hind end rounded; lower margin straight, with gap between valves for byssus; beaks small, at front end, pointed downward. Exterior purplish-gray, covered by smooth dark brown skin; sculptured with many radiating, flattened ridges. Interior grayish-white, with 2 small teeth near beaks.

Range Alaska to central Mexico.

Habitat Attached to rocks, from between tide lines to water 150′ deep.

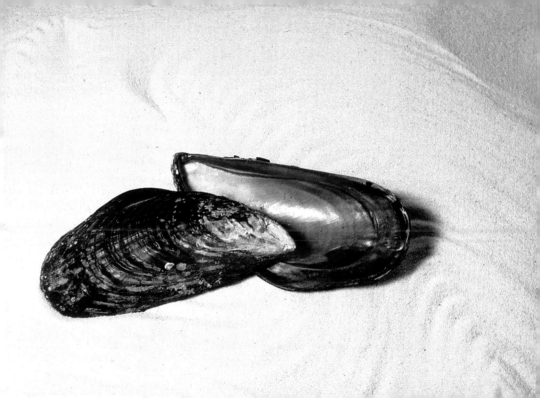

Ribbed Mussel *Geukensia demissa*

This mussel is very abundant in the salt marshes and estuaries of the Middle Atlantic and the southeastern states. Like many other bivalves, mussels obtain food by filtering the seawater as it passes over their gills to strain out minute organisms and food particles, which are then passed to the mouth by the wavelike motions of tiny, hairlike cilia.

Identification
$2\frac{1}{2}$–$6\frac{3}{4}$″ long. Elongately ovate or fan-shaped, rather thin-shelled, beaks a short distance behind bluntly rounded front end. Exterior with shiny olive-brown to dark brown skin; sculptured with crowded radial riblets that are larger near upper margin. No teeth inside front end of hinge margin.

Similar Species
Granular-ribbed Mussel (*G. d. granosissima*), 2–$4\frac{3}{4}$″ long, a subspecies found from Florida to Mexico, is larger, more slender, with more numerous and beaded riblets.

Range
Gulf of St. Lawrence, Canada, to N.E. Florida.

Habitat
Buried in mud or peat in salt marshes or bays.

Flat-tipped Piddock *Penitella penita*

The most abundant piddock on the West Coast, the Flat-tipped is considered delicious eating and is collected for that reason. In this and some other species, the foot emerges through a large gap in the front, especially in young; in older specimens this gap is partially or wholly closed by extensions of the valves and the piddock, resting in its now-completed "home," no longer bores.

Identification   1¼–3″ long. Moderately large, elongately ovate, front part inflated, divided by diagonal groove from elongated, somewhat flattened hind part. Beaks halfway between middle and front end; shelly extension of front end extends over beaks and front part of upper margin. Exterior whitish, with crowded, scaly concentric ridges in front; hind part with concentric wrinkles, fibrous skin, and leathery extensions at valve ends.

Range   Alaska to central Baja California.

Habitat   In clay and soft rock, from low-tide line to water 70′ deep.

Pilsbry Piddock *Zirfaea pilsbryi*

The piddock family is a group of bivalves that bore into all sorts of substances from wood to plastic. This species belongs to a genus in which the animals are big and have shells that gape greatly at both the front (for the foot) and the hind end (for the very large siphons). The valves touch only in the beak area of the upper margin and along two-thirds of the lower margin.

Identification 2–4¾″ long. Oblong-ovate, inflated, with an angle above front gap; hind end rounded. Exterior dull white to pale salmon. Groove from beaks to lower margin, hind part relatively smooth, front half with strong, erect concentric ridges crossed in front quarter by strong, radial ridges that are scaly or spiny at intersection. Interior white, with elongate, spoon-shaped projection under each beak; front part of lower margin spiny.

Range Central Alaska to S. Baja California.

Habitat In mud and clay banks, in shallow water.

Angel Wing *Cyrtopleura costata*

Common on the west coast of Florida, the Angel Wing is collected for food, and the shell is prized by collectors. Other members of the piddock family can bore into wood, rock, and even lead or plastic cables. The Angel Wing bores into mud or clay by using scaly ridges along the front end of the shell, which it rocks back and forth with the foot and the muscles that hold the shell together. Chemicals excreted from glands may assist some species in boring into harder substances.

Identification 4–8″ long. Elongately ovate, front end rounded, hind end narrowed; usually white, sometimes tinged with pink. Exterior with scaly radial ridges, those at front end sharply angular, those behind beaks more flattened; upper margin at front end expanded and curved over beaks. Interior white, with broad, spoon-shaped projection originating under beaks.

Range S. Massachusetts to N. West Indies and Brazil.

Habitat In deep, sandy mud or clay, at or just below low-tide line to water 60′ deep.

False Angel Wing *Petricola pholadiformis*

As its name indicates, this boring clam resembles the true Angel Wing, but it is smaller, with small teeth under the beaks and no accessory shelly structures near the beak area. Related to the venus clam family, the False Angel Wing and its kin all bore in heavy mud, peat, rock, coral, or damp wood, or find a settling place in holes or crevices. Because of this habit the shells often become deformed or irregular in shape.

Identification 1½–2¼″ long. Elongately cylindrical, thin-shelled, front end inflated but becoming more compressed toward rear end; beaks a short distance behind front end. Exterior whitish; front end with low, scaly riblets that become finer; no scales on rest of shell. Interior white; front-end riblets visible as grooves; 2 small teeth under beak of right valve.

Range Gulf of St. Lawrence, Canada, to Texas; also introduced into California and Washington, as well as Europe.

Habitat In heavy mud, peat, or clay, between tide lines.

118

Zebra Ark *Arca zebra*

This member of the ark family is also known as the Turkey Wing because of the dark zigzag streaks on the shell. The species nestles in crevices in coral and rock, where it attaches itself by means of a byssus, a bundle of horny threads that emerges through a gap in the lower part of the shell.

Identification 1¾–3½″ long. Broadly oblong, boxlike, valves inflated, with beaks separated by a broad flattened area; distance from front end to beaks ¼ of total length. Valves with angled ridge from beaks to lower part of hind end; sculptured with many radial ridges. Yellowish-white or pale brown, with reddish-brown zigzag bands; has matted brown skin when fresh. Hinge line straight, with many fine teeth.

Range North Carolina to Brazil.

Habitat In crevices and hollows of coral or rock, from low-tide line to water 40′ deep.

Ponderous Ark *Noetia ponderosa*

Fossil specimens of this thick-shelled species are found on beaches north of where it now lives. Washed out of ancient sandy deposits up to 300,000 years old, the fossils are proof that the waters were warmer then. Like most of the sand- and mud-dwelling arks, this shell has strongly toothed and scalloped margins so that the valves interlock when closed.

Identification 1½–2¾″ long. Heavy, thick-shelled, roughly triangular in outline. Strongly angled from beaks to lower part of hind end; beaks large, in middle of hinge line, turned toward hind end; area between beaks moderately broad. Exterior whitish, covered with thick, feltlike, dark brown skin and sculptured with strong, flattened radial ribs.

Range Virginia to Texas.

Habitat In sand, from just below the low-tide line to water 60′ deep.

Blood Ark *Anadara ovalis*

This species gets its name from the fact that its blood is red, due to the presence of hemoglobin; most other mollusks have clear blood. The Blood Ark, like many other members of its family, buries itself in sand. The young have a single byssus or fiber, by which they attach themselves to a pebble; later in life this fiber is lost, as is the gap between the shell's valves through which it emerges.

Identification 1–3″ long. Broadly oval to almost round; beaks close together, separated by narrow, V-shaped depression. Valves inflated, whitish or pale yellowish, usually covered by a thick, fibrous, dark brown skin (periostracum); sculptured with many flattened radial ridges, which may be grooved. Interior white; hinge line below beaks curved, with about 37 small teeth.

Range Cape Cod, Massachusetts, to Brazil.

Habitat In sand and mud, from low-tide line to water 10′ deep.

Pacific Littleneck *Protothaca staminea*

The Pacific Littleneck, a member of the venus clam family, is one of the commercially important food clams fished along the Pacific Coast. Because it is smaller than the Washington Clam, it is not used much in the canning industry but is sold fresh in markets.

Identification 1½–2⅜″ long. Broadly ovate to almost oblong, moderately inflated, beaks between middle and front end. Exterior yellowish-white or brownish, sometimes with large brownish splotches, zigzag markings, or spots; many axial ribs, broadest on hind slope; ridges on front slope with beaded concentric ridges crowded near margin; ridges on hind half crossed by irregular growth lines.

Similar Species Japanese Littleneck (*Tapes philippinarum*), 1½–2″ long, is more elongate and compressed; introduced to California.

Range Central Alaska to S. Baja California.

Habitat In lower half of intertidal zone, in coarse, sandy mud or muddy gravel in bays, or in gravel on open coasts.

Nuttall Cockle *Clinocardium nuttallii*

The cockle family is a large group with many species that are of commercial importance as food, particularly in Europe. Our species, fished commercially in Puget Sound, is used primarily as bait, but it is said that the meat makes a fine chowder. Cockles have a strong, narrow, sickle-shaped foot that they use to dig themselves into the sand or move across the sand by leaps.

Identification   2–5½″ high. Broadly ovate to almost circular, moderately inflated, beaks curved forward and in front of middle. Exterior grayish with a thin, tough, light brown skin, sometimes with dark concentric bands; sculptured with many flattened ribs with transverse beads; beads absent on narrow ribs at hind end. Interior yellowish to white; margin strongly scalloped.

Range   Bering Sea to San Diego, California.

Habitat   In sand or mud, from between tide lines to water 1,080′ deep.

128

Alaska Jingle *Pododesmus macrochisma*

Sometimes called the False Pacific Jingle, this is the largest jingle shell found in North American waters, if not in the whole world. Native Americans collected it for food, and Eskimos still eat this jingle in Alaska, where it is very abundant.

Identification 1–4″ high. Irregularly circular to broadly ovate, moderately thick-shelled; hole for byssus closed at margin of attached valve in fully grown adults. Exterior grayish-white, sometimes tinged with green; with irregular ribs, usually coarsely wrinkled by irregular growth lines. Interior greenish, sometimes brownish, with irregular white splotches; free valve with 1 large and 1 small muscle scar.

Similar Species Abalone Jingle (*P. cepio*), 1½–3¾″ high; thinner with finer ribbing; S. Alaska to Baja California.

Range Arctic Ocean to S. Alaska.

Habitat On rocks, pilings, and shells, from low-tide line to water 200′ deep.

Common Eastern Jingle *Anomia simplex*

Jingles are thin, often translucent shells whose lower valve has a hole through which the large byssus attaches to rocks, other shells, or wood. At the point of attachment, the byssus may become more or less calcified. The upper valve is frequently washed up on beaches; handfuls of the thin, shiny golden or silvery shells shaken together make a characteristic jingling sound.

Identification ¾–2¼″ long. Irregularly circular to ovate. Upper valve slightly convex, thin, somewhat shiny; yellowish, orange, or silvery white, irregularly wrinkled or smooth. Interior pearly except for dull white oval area at center and 3 small muscle scars. Lower valve very thin, attached, with hole for byssus and a round muscle scar.

Range S. Massachusetts to Brazil.

Habitat On rocks, shells, or wood, from near low-tide line to water 30′ deep.

Eastern Oyster *Crassostrea virginica*

Members of the oyster family are more widely used as food than any other bivalve group. Oysters begin life as males, change their sex several times, and end up as females. A single oyster may lay millions of eggs during one spawning season, but only a few of these will reach maturity. The swimming larvae, which begin crawling about in one to three weeks, finally attach themselves to rock, wood, or other shells.

Identification 2–8″ long. Shape variable, usually elongate but also broadly ovate. Thick-shelled, upper valve smaller and flatter than lower attached valve. Grayish or yellowish-white, sometimes with purple rays; smooth except for wrinkles, irregular platelike growth ridges, or radial ridges, especially on lower valve. Interior white with purple oval muscle scar and strong, triangular, horny ligament at narrowed top.

Range Maryland to Gulf of Mexico.

Habitat On hard or soft bottom, often in clusters, from low-tide line to water 40′ deep.

134

Olympia Oyster *Ostrea lurida*

This species is also known as the Native or Yaquina Oyster. Although it is considerably smaller than the Giant Pacific Oyster or the Eastern Oyster, many people claim that the Olympia is far tastier than the others. Like them, it is cultivated commercially, but not as extensively.

Identification 1½–3½″ long. Irregular; in general, broadly ovate, usually more or less narrowed at upper end. Attached lower valve concave, upper valve flatter. Exterior grayish-white to purplish-brown, occasionally with dark rays; wrinkled or with scaly growth lines, and sometimes with angled radial ridges that make margin fluted. Interior grayish-white, often tinged with green. Fine teeth in upper valve on each side of beak, corresponding pits in other valve.

Range S. Alaska to S. Baja California.

Habitat On rocks near low-tide line, or in beds on mud flats or gravel beds in bays.

Giant Pacific Oyster *Crassostrea gigas*

The Giant Pacific was first imported from Japan about 1912 in the form of very young oysters called seed oysters or spat. These are still occasionally brought in from Japan, but now most of the spat is raised commercially in Washington and British Columbia. This large species is the principal commercial oyster on our Northwest Coast.

Identification 2–12″ long. Large, broadly ovate to somewhat elongate, narrowed at upper end. Exterior grayish-white, occasionally with dark spots, strongly ridged; margin angularly scalloped. Interior white with oval muscle scar that is white or tinged with purplish-brown; margin smooth.

Range S. Alaska to N. California; also Japan.

Habitat Between tide lines, on rock, sand, gravel, or mud.

Atlantic Bay Scallop *Argopecten irradians*

The scallop family contains some of the most important commercially fished bivalves. Only the large central muscle is eaten. Marine grasses and other plants play a key role in the life of scallops: The young swimming larvae attach themselves by a byssus to leaves and stems, and then when almost an inch long, drop to the bottom. Many species retain the byssus as adults, fastening themselves to coral, rocks, or other objects, but some can swim to escape such predators as starfish.

Identification 1½–4″ long. Valve moderately inflated, almost circular in outline, with small, triangular, winglike projections on each side of pointed beaks. Valves white to dark gray or brown, often with concentric color bands or radial rays; lower valve often lighter than upper; sculptured with 17–18 rounded ribs that are angular at margin.

Range Massachusetts to New Jersey.

Habitat In muddy sand, near eelgrass, and in water 1–60′ deep.

Cross-barred Venus *Chione cancellata*

The Cross-barred Venus, abundant in Florida, is a member of the large venus clam family, a group of rather thick-shelled, sculptured or strikingly colored species with strong hinge teeth. The animal uses its strong, triangular foot to dig itself into sand or mud. Many of the larger species are used as food and some are fished commercially.

Identification 1–1¾" long. Broadly ovate to almost triangular; beaks prominent, pointed forward; upper side with smooth, heart-shaped depression in front of beaks and narrow, spearhead-shaped depression behind beaks. Exterior whitish, sometimes with brown rays, with many curving radial ridges crossed by strong, erect, concentric ridges that are wavy at intersection. Interior whitish, suffused with purple; margins grooved and toothed.

Range North Carolina to Brazil.

Habitat In sand, from between tide lines to water 60′ deep.

Washington Clam *Saxidomus nuttalli*

The common name Washington Clam is a misnomer, as this species does not occur in the state of Washington. Known locally as the Butter Clam, it is an esteemed food and is fished for extensively, especially in northern California.

Identification   2¾–4¾″ long. Oblong-ovate, moderately inflated, thick-shelled, gaping at hind end. Exterior grayish-yellow to brownish, often with rust-brown splotches; fine but strong, irregular, concentric ridges crowded near front end, erect and platelike at hind end. Interior white, stained with purple at hind end.

Similar Species   Smooth Washington Clam (*S. giganteus*), 2½–4″ long, is white, slightly higher, and smoother, and is also an important, commercially harvested food; central California to S. Alaska.

Range   N. California to N. Baja California.

Habitat   Deep in sand in bays or offshore, from near low-tide line to water 150′ deep.

Northern Quahog *Mercenaria mercenaria*

Quahog is the Algonquian name for this large species, a commercially important food known also as the Littleneck or Hardshelled Clam. Native Americans ate the flesh and fashioned the shell into tools and ornaments. Beads cut from the shell were strung together and used as money called wampum; those cut from the purple part of the inside were considered more valuable.

Identification 2¾–4¼″ long. Large, broadly ovate, thick-shelled, beaks large, near front end. Exterior grayish-yellow, often with brownish tinge; fine, erect concentric ridges over most of shell except for smooth area near center of each valve. Interior white, usually with a purple spot near hind end; margin finely toothed.

Range Gulf of St. Lawrence to Texas.

Habitat In sand or mud in bays and inlets, from between tide lines to water 50′ deep.

Atlantic Surfclam *Spisula solidissima*

On Cape Cod this species is made into a delicious clam pie. Also known as the Beach, Skimmer, or Hen Clam, it is a commercially important member of the surfclam family. The shells of this group are characterized by a shelflike hinge under the beaks, where a triangular or oval depression holds a stout horny pad called the resilium, a feature that in living surfclams works against the muscles that close the valves to allow the clam to take in water and food.

Identification 1¾–7″ long. Oval, moderately inflated, with hind end bluntly angled and front end rounded; beaks prominent, just in front of middle. Exterior smooth, yellowish-white, covered with a thin, yellowish-brown skin that is fibrous at hind end. Interior white to cream-colored; muscle scars at each end, connected by a line marking attachment of mantle to shell.

Range Nova Scotia to South Carolina.

Habitat In sand, from just below low-tide line to water 140′ deep.

Hemphill Surfclam *Spisula hemphilli*

A fairly common surfclam, this species is somewhat higher and less elongate than the Atlantic Surfclam. Like that relative, it is considered delicious eating but is gathered only incidentally by diggers searching for other kinds of clams.

Identification 2½–6″ long. Large, oval; beaks near middle, elevated, bent slightly forward; front part of upper margin concave, hind part convex. Exterior yellowish-white, with thin brown skin, skin wrinkled near hind end, forming concentric lines. Surface relatively smooth; strong, angled ridge runs from beaks to lower end of hind margin. Interior dull white, shiny along margin.

Range Santa Barbara, California, to N. Baja California.

Habitat In sand or sandy mud, from low-tide line to water 150′ deep.

Pismo Clam *Tivela stultorum*

The largest of the venus clams found on our Pacific Coast, the Pismo has been a major edible clam for many years; in 1923 it ranked first among clams in importance. The shell is named for Pismo Beach, near San Luis Obispo, California, where it was formerly abundant. A decline in its numbers has brought about strict harvesting controls: a bag limit, minimum legal size, and no summer or commercial fishing. The Pismo Clam takes seven years to grow to five inches.

Identification 3–6¼″ long. Large, very thick-shelled, ovate-triangular. Beaks large, near center; rounded angle from beaks to lower part of bluntly rounded hind end; front end evenly rounded. Exterior whitish, often with purplish radial rays; essentially smooth, with a thin, shiny, yellowish-brown skin. Interior white or cream-colored. Hinge area heavy, with strong teeth.

Range Monterey, California, to central Mexico.

Habitat In sand, between tide lines to water 40′ deep.

Baltic Macoma *Macoma balthica*

The Baltic Macoma belongs to the large tellin family, whose members have flattened, usually ovate to almost round shells. They live buried in sand or sandy mud, lying horizontally on the left valve with one long siphon protruding from the sand into the water, taking in water and food. The shorter other siphon reaches just to the surface of the sand and discharges water and wastes.

Identification   ¾–1½″ long. Broadly oval, rather flattened and thin-shelled; front end rounded, hind end slightly narrowed, beaks near center of upper edge. Exterior white, with a thin, pale grayish-white skin that is usually partly rubbed off; irregular concentric growth ridges. Interior white, shiny, with 2 small teeth under beaks in each valve.

Range   Arctic seas to Georgia; also Alaska and N. Europe.

Habitat   In mud, muddy sand, or gravel, from between tide lines to water 35′ deep; in deeper water farther south.

Softshell Clam *Mya arenaria*

A member of a small family found mostly in cold, northern waters, this species is also known as the Steamer Clam, and as the Long-neck Clam because of its long siphons and surrounding flexible casing. An important food, this clam is especially prized along the New England Coast, where fried or steamed it is considered a delicacy. In about 1865 or 1870 it was introduced into California.

Identification 1–5½″ long. Ovate, moderately thin-shelled; front end rounded, hind end narrowed, beaks near center. Exterior grayish-white, covered with a thin, light brown skin; irregular growth lines and ridges. Interior white, with horny pad, or resilium, on horizontally projecting shelf in left valve; right valve with horny pad in depression under beak.

Range Labrador to North Carolina, and British Columbia to California; also in Europe.

Habitat In sand and mud, from between tide lines to water 240′ deep.

156

Bentnose Macoma *Macoma nasuta*

Members of the tellin family, macoma clams differ from true tellins in that they lack internal teeth on either side of their beaks. They are usually dull white, and for the most part are found in sand or mud in quiet bays. This species is also known as the Oyster Clam because its flavor supposedly resembles that of an oyster. It is considered excellent eating in some localities.

Identification   1¼–3¼″ long. Broadly ovate, shell moderately thick; front end rounded, hind end narrowed and twisted; beaks in middle. Right valve with broad ridge running from beak to lower hind end. Exterior yellowish-white or grayish-white, with thin, fibrous, yellowish-brown skin; smooth, with irregular wrinkles or growth lines. Interior white; 2 teeth under beak in right valve, 1 in left valve.

Range   Central Alaska to S. Baja California.

Habitat   In sandy mud in bays and estuaries, from between tide lines to deeper waters.

Geoduck *Panope abrupta*

The largest clam in American waters, the Geoduck may weigh as much as eight pounds. It lives two to four feet below the surface. Its siphons, which are united and cannot be withdrawn into the shell, reach a length of three feet or more. Geoducks are excellent eating, and overharvested in some areas. To conserve these clams, a few states have a daily limit of three. Geoducks belong to the gaper family.

Identification 3½–9″ long. Large, oblong, front end rounded, hind end squared off. Beaks near middle of upper margin, which is almost straight; lower margin straight or slightly curved; valves gape everywhere except at beaks. Exterior grayish-white to yellowish-white, with a thin, yellowish-brown skin and strong, irregular growth wrinkles. Interior whitish, with small tooth under each beak and strong platform for the horny ligament.

Range S. Alaska to central Baja California.

Habitat In sandy mud in bays, from between tide lines to water 50′ deep.

Pacific Gaper *Tresus nuttalli*

The Pacific Gaper is a large surfclam noted for its long, united siphons. This clam lives in the sand, one to three feet below the surface. As the animal withdraws its siphons, the water they release may squirt several feet high, thus revealing the presence of a live gaper beneath the sand. The Pacific Gaper is highly prized for its delicious flavor.

Identification 5½–7½" long. Large, oblong-oval, thin-shelled for its size; inflated, beaks large, in front of middle. Hind end broad, rounded, with large gap for siphons. Exterior yellowish-white, covered with brown skin, fibrous near margins. Smooth except for growth lines. Interior white; teeth under beaks weak.

Similar Species Alaskan Gaper (*T. capax*), 6–10" long, is larger, more inflated, and oval, with a rounded lower margin; Alaska to Monterey, California.

Range Puget Sound to central Baja California.

Habitat In sand, from low-tide line to water 100' deep.

162

White Sand Macoma *Macoma secta*

This large macoma makes for excellent eating and is often available in markets and restaurants. Unlike the Bentnose Macoma, it lives in more sandy areas and near entrances to bays. As in other members of the tellin family, the siphons are long and separate. Shells in this group have a tendency to become clogged with mud or sand, so to clean them, keep them alive in running seawater for a while.

Identification 2–4½″ long. Large, broadly ovate, moderately thin-shelled. Left valve usually flatter than right valve; hind margin with raised, convex, flattened extension; beaks in middle, with low ridge running from beaks to hind end in right valve. Exterior pale yellowish-white to white, smooth except for fine growth lines. Interior white, with short, oblique ridge from beaks in each valve.

Range Vancouver Island, British Columbia, to central Baja California.

Habitat In sandy areas, from between tide lines to deeper water.

164

Amethyst Clam *Gemma gemma*

This shell, a member of the venus clam family, is easily recognized by its small size and purple color. The female develops fertilized eggs between its mantle folds; from there, they are released as young ready to burrow in mud or sand. Both young and adults are prey to ducks, fish, and various invertebrates such as moonsnails, crabs, and a species of burrowing sea anemone.

Identification   ⅛″ long. Very small, inflated, beaks near center. Exterior yellowish or grayish-white, usually tinged with pale purple, or purplish with pale margin; shiny with fine growth lines or wrinkles. Interior tinged with purple.

Range   Nova Scotia to Texas and Bahamas; also introduced to Pacific Coast, occurring in Puget Sound.

Habitat   On sand or mud flats, above low-tide line.

166

Candystick Tellin *Tellina similis*

This species is one of a group of warm-water tellins with rather small, thin shells that are tinted or colored. The Candystick Tellin gets its name from the pink rays often found on the shell. In the tellins, the sexes are separate and fertilization occurs in the water. After hatching, the young actively swim in the ocean, but as adults, they burrow and do not swim.

Identification   ⅝–1⅛″ long. Oblong-ovate, shiny, rather thin-shelled; beaks behind middle, front end broadly rounded. Exterior white or pale yellow, flushed with pink or with pink rays near lower margin; fine concentric ridges crossed in middle by oblique grooves. Interior white, yellowish, or flushed or rayed with pink.

Similar Species   Rainbow Tellin (*T. iris*), ⅜–½″ long, is smaller, thin, and translucent, and with more distant, often obscure, oblique grooves; North Carolina to Texas.

Range   South Carolina to Brazil.

Habitat   In sand, from between tide lines to water 150′ deep.

Coquina *Donax variabilis*

This colorful little shell is a member of the wedgeclam family. Very abundant on some sandy beaches, they are quite active, burrowing in the sand between tides. If exposed after a retreating wave, these shells will quickly dig themselves back into the wet sand. Not only are they the basis of a famous chowder, but also these attractive bivalves are used in shellcraft. Since Colonial times beds of compacted dead Coquina shells, known as coquina rock, have been a source of building material.

Identification   ½–1″ long. Small, comparatively thick-shelled, elongately triangular; front end long, rounded, hind end slightly angled. Exterior whitish, usually suffused, rayed, or banded with purple, pink, orange, yellow, brown, or blue; smooth except for fine radial ridges, especially on hind portion. Interior variously colored, with margins strongly grooved and toothed.

Range   New York to N. Mexico.

Habitat   In sand, from between tide lines to low-tide line.

Northern Pacific Razorclam *Siliqua patula*

This, the largest representative of the American jackknife clam family, is eagerly sought after by clam diggers on the beaches of our Northwest Coast, especially in northern Oregon and Washington. It is a good eating clam and is also harvested commercially. The Northern Pacific Razorclam is a challenge to dig for because it can burrow itself rapidly in the wet sand. Unlike some other species in its family, this one does not inhabit permanent burrows.

Identification 3–6¼" long. Large, elongately oblong, compressed, rather thin-shelled; front end rounded, hind end somewhat squared off; beaks about halfway between middle and front end. Exterior grayish-white, smooth; skin tough, thin, brown to olive-green. Interior whitish, faintly flushed with purple, with low, gradually widening white ridge from below beaks to lower margin.

Range S. Alaska to Monterey, California.

Habitat In sand on ocean beaches, between tide lines.

172

California Tagelus *Tagelus californianus*

Also called the California Jackknife Clam because it resembles some razorclams, this species belongs to the sandclam family. These shells have beaks near the center of the upper margin rather than at or near the front end. The California Tagelus lives in permanent burrows; it keeps the ends of its siphons a short distance above the bottom surface, so it can take in matter suspended in the water.

Identification 1¾–4¼″ long. Elongately oblong, with upper and lower margins almost parallel; beaks central, with a groove from beaks to middle of hind end; area above it somewhat flattened. Exterior whitish or yellowish, often with incised, reddish-brown vertical lines in central area; skin thin, yellowish, thicker and fibrous near hind end.

Range S. Oregon to central Mexico.

Habitat In sandy mud in bays, between tide lines.

174

Rosy Jackknife Clam *Solen rosaceus*

An abundant razorclam on the California Coast, this species, like some others in the family, occupies a permanent burrow. The clam moves up and down by opening and closing its valves; when the animal's body expands or contracts it pushes the valves against the sides of the burrow, and simultaneously causes its foot to expand or contract, pushing the shell up or down in the sand.

Identification 1½–3″ long. Elongately ovate, almost 5 times as long as high; front end straight, inclined forward, hind end rounded and slightly narrowed; upper and lower margins straight, parallel. Exterior white, often pink-tinged, skin grayish-green, thin, shiny, smooth. Interior white, flushed with pink; 1 tooth under each beak.

Range Santa Barbara, California, to central Mexico.

Habitat In bays, in sand at low-tide line and deeper.

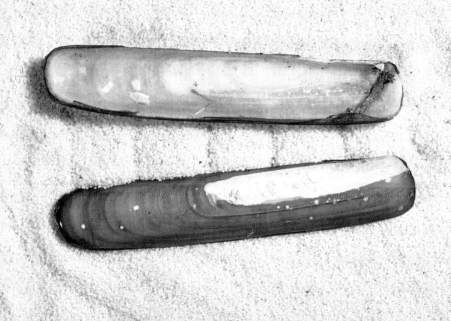

Atlantic Jackknife Clam *Ensis directus*

Jackknife clams are elongate, flattened bivalves with parallel or broadly oblong sides. Endowed with a muscular foot, they are strong diggers in sand or mud and are active swimmers. The larger species, like this one, are edible, and some are fished commercially. The Atlantic Jackknife Clam was formerly sold in markets along the northeastern Atlantic Coast.

Identification   3–8″ long. Narrowly oblong, slightly curved, with parallel sides; both ends squared off, front end rounded at lower corner. Beaks at front end; low, flattened, gradually widening ridge runs from there to rear end. Exterior with thin olive-green skin, grayish on flat ridge; smooth except for fine growth lines. Interior bluish-white; small teeth under beaks.

Similar Species   Minor Jackknife Clam (*E. minor*), 1¾–4½″ long, is smaller, more slender, and paler; New Jersey to Texas.

Range   Labrador to South Carolina.

Habitat   In sand, between tide lines.

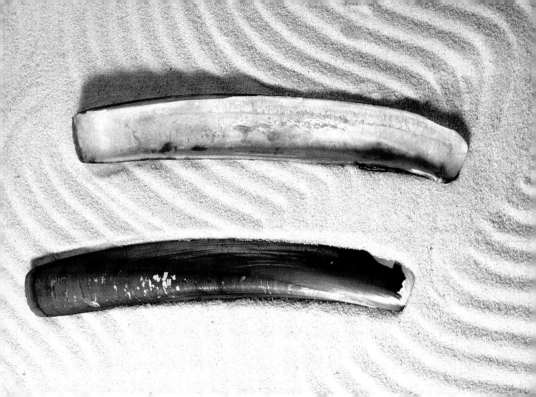

Shell Groups

Abalones, family Haliotidae
pages 92–94

Arks, family Arcidae
pages 120–124

Crown Conchs, family
Melongenidae
page 50

Dogwinkles, family Thaididae
pages 28, 34, 52

Chitons, class Polyplacophora
pages 88–90

Cockles, family Cardiidae
page 128

Cones, family Conidae
page 24

Dovesnails, family Columbellidae
page 66

Helmet Snails, family Cassidae
page 26

Hornsnails, family Potamididae
page 64

Jackknife Clams, family
Cultellidae
pages 172, 178

Jingles, family Anomiidae
pages 130–132

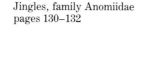

Keyhole Limpets, family
Fissurellidae
page 96

Mussels, family Mytilidae
pages 106–110

Nerites, family Neritidae
page 76

Olive Shells, family Olividae
pages 20–22

Limpets, family Acmaeidae
pages 98–104

Moonsnails, family Naticidae
pages 80–84

Murex Snails, family Muricidae
pages 54–60

Oysters, family Ostreidae
pages 134–138

Periwinkles, family Littorinidae
pages 68–70, 74

Piddocks, family Pholadidae, and
False Angel Wings, family
Petricolidae
pages 112–118

Razorclams, family Solenidae
page 176

Scallops, family Pectinidae
page 140

Slippershells, family Crepidulidae
page 86

Tellins, family Tellinidae,
Sandclams, family Solecurtidae,
Wedgeclams, family Donacidae
pages 154, 158, 164, 168–170, 174

Topsnails, family Trochidae
pages 72, 78

Venus Clams, family Veneridae
pages 126, 142–146, 152, 166

Softshell Clams, family Myidae, and Gapers, family Hiatellidae
page 156, 160–162

Spindle Shells, family Fasciolariidae
page 38

Surfclams, family Mactridae
pages 148–150

Wentletraps, family Epitoniidae
page 62

Whelks, family Buccinidae, and Dog Whelks, family Nassariidae
page 30–32, 36, 40–44

Wing Conchs, family Strombidae
pages 46–48

Glossary

Aperture
In gastropods, the opening for the head and foot.

Apex
The tip of a gastropod's shell, comprising the smallest whorls. (Adjective, apical)

Axis
In gastropods, an imaginary line running parallel to the shell's axis, or from apex to base. (Adjective, axial)

Beak
In bivalves, the earliest part of the shell.

Body whorl
In gastropods, the last full turn of a spiral shell, including the aperture.

Byssus
The tough chitin fibers secreted by some bivalves and which anchor them to objects.

Canal
In gastropods, an open channel or a tube at the base of the shell, containing the animal's siphons.

Girdle
In chitons, a band of muscular tissue that surrounds the valves and holds them together.

Hinge area
In bivalves, the inside of the beak, with interlocking teeth and pits that help to keep the valves aligned.

Hinge ligament
An elongated horny element at the hinge, either external or internal, that holds the valves together.

Intertidal zone
The area between high- and low-tide lines.

Larva
The youngest stage of a mollusk.

Mantle
The fleshy fold (or folds) that surrounds the vital organs of a living mollusk and contains glands that secrete the shell.

Operculum
A shelly or horny plate that wholly or partly closes the aperture when a gastropod withdraws into its shell.

Oval
Evenly elliptical, with both ends equally curved.

Ovate
Elliptical but with one end broader than the other; egg-shaped.

Pad
In gastropods, a thickening on the shell, also called a callus. In certain bivalves, a horny cushion found in the hinge area, also called the resilium.

Radial
In bivalves, running outward from the apex of a valve.

Radula
An organ in the mouth cavity of gastropods and chitons consisting of minute teeth, usually on a flexible ribbon, used in feeding.

Resilium
A cartilaginous pad, elastic in living bivalves, that is found in a depression in the hinge area.

Ribs
The ridgelike sculptural elements that are axial in gastropods, radial in bivalves.

Shoulder
In gastropods, the flattened part of each whorl, below the suture.

Siphon
A tubelike extension of the mantle that carries water, food particles, and waste products in or out of the mantle cavity.

Spiral
A sculpture or color pattern that follows the spiral turns of a snail shell.

Spire
In gastropods, all whorls above the aperture or body whorl.

Suture
The line or space that separates adjoining turns of a spiral shell.

Teeth
In gastropods, short protuberances generally found on the margin or inside the outer lip; in bivalves, shelly protuberances of various sizes and shapes in the hinge area.

Turreted
Having whorls that form a high, conical spire.

Umbilicus
The opening of the hollow axis in the base of some snail shells.

Valve
In bivalves, one of two parts of the shell; in chitons, one of eight plates.

Whorl
In gastropods, one of the full coils of the shell.

Index

Numbers in italics refer to shells mentioned as similar species.

**Prepared and produced by
Chanticleer Press, Inc.**

Founding Publisher: Paul Steiner
Publisher: Andrew Stewart

Staff for this book:

Editor-in-Chief: Gudrun Buettner
Executive Editor: Susan Costello
Managing Editor: Jane Opper
Natural Science Editor: John
Farrand, Jr.
Assistant Editor: Amy K Hughes
Production Manager: Helga Lose
Production: Gina Stead-Thomas,
Helen L.A. Brown
Art Direction: Carol Nehring
Art Associates: Ayn Svoboda,
Cheryl Miller
Picture Library: Edward Douglas
Original series design by
Massimo Vignelli.

All editorial inquiries should be
addressed to:
Chanticleer Press
665 Broadway, Suite 1001
New York, NY 10012
www.eNature.com

To purchase this book or other
National Audubon Society
illustrated nature books, please
contact:
Alfred A. Knopf, Inc.
299 Park Ave.
New York, NY 10171
(800) 733-3000
www.randomhouse.com

NATIONAL AUDUBON SOCIETY

The mission of NATIONAL AUDUBON SOCIETY *is to conserve and restore natural ecosystems, focusing on birds, other wildlife, and their habitats for the benefit of humanity and the earth's biological diversity.*

One of the largest environmental organizations, AUDUBON has 550,000 members, 100 sanctuaries and nature centers, and 508 chapters in the Americas, plus a professional staff of scientists, lobbyists, lawyers, policy analysts, and educators.

Award-winning *Audubon* magazine, sent to all members, carries outstanding articles and color photography on wildlife, nature, the environment, and conservation. Audubon also publishes *Audubon Adventures*, a children's newspaper reaching 450,000 students. We offer professional development for educators and activists through ecology camps and workshops in Maine, Connecticut, and Wyoming, plus unique, traveling undergraduate and graduate degree programs through *Audubon Expedition Institute*.

AUDUBON sponsors books, CD-ROMs, and travel programs to exotic places like Antarctica, Africa, Australia, Baja California, and the Galápagos Islands. For information about how to become a member, to subscribe to *Audubon Adventures*, or to learn more about our camps and workshops, please contact us at:

NATIONAL AUDUBON SOCIETY
Membership Dept.
700 Broadway, New York, NY 10003-9562
(800) 274-4201 or (212) 979-3000
http://www.audubon.org/